HARLAND LEARNS TO DRAW

3-D

By: Brian Lemay

Editor: Margaret Wood

Cyril Hayes Press Inc.
3312 Mainway, Burlington, Ontario L7M 1A7
One Colomba Drive, Niagara Falls,
New York 14305

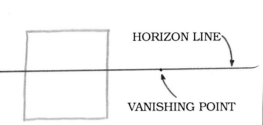

HORIZON LINE

VANISHING POINT

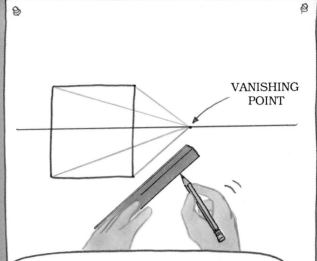

VANISHING POINT

This time let's try the same thing, but put the vanishing point outside the square.

Now, draw the lines from each corner of the box to the vanishing point using your ruler.

And, just as we did in our last drawing, draw another square inside the first one.

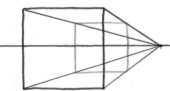

Don't forget to make sure the corners connect to the lines going to the vanishing point.

Go over your box with your pencil again to clean it up a little.

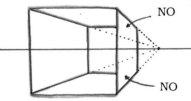

NO

NO

Don't finish off these two lines. This way it looks like that side of the box is solid and you can't see through it.

Finally, erase the horizon line and the lines outside the box that go to the vanishing point.

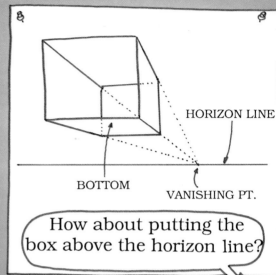

HORIZON LINE

BOTTOM

VANISHING PT.

How about putting the box above the horizon line?

That makes it look like you can see underneath the box.

Exactly!

If you put the box below the horizon line, it's as if you're looking at the top of it.

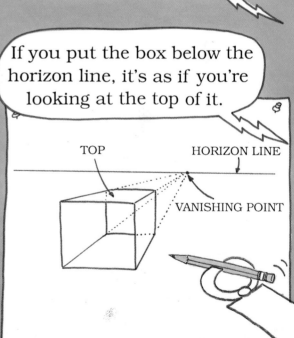

TOP

HORIZON LINE

VANISHING POINT

Oh, I understand! The horizon line is at my eye level.

That's right. Let's try something else now.

HORIZON LINE

VANISHING PT. 1

VANISHING PT. 2

Draw your horizon line and pick two vanishing points at either end of the paper on the horizon line.

Draw a short line up and down that crosses the horizon line.

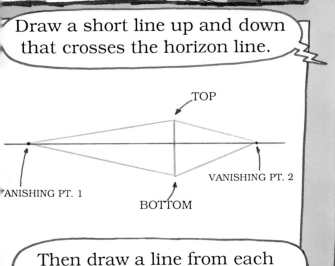

TOP

VANISHING PT. 2

VANISHING PT. 1

BOTTOM

Then draw a line from each vanishing point to the ends of the line.

Now draw two more lines like this to finish off your box.

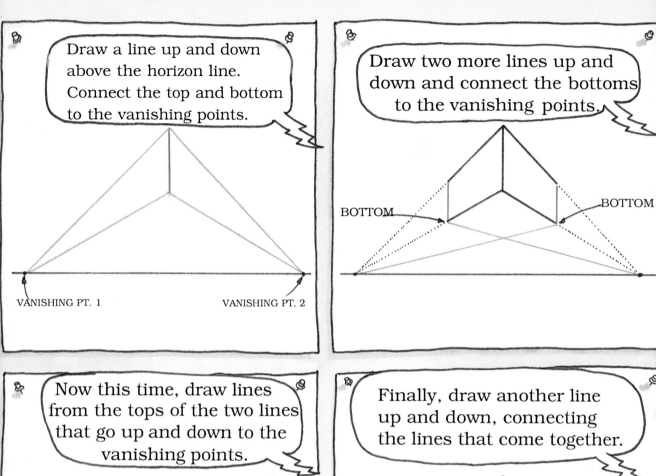

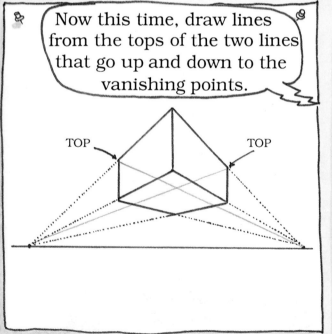

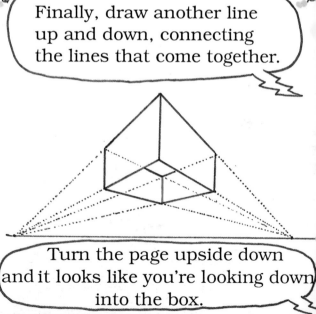

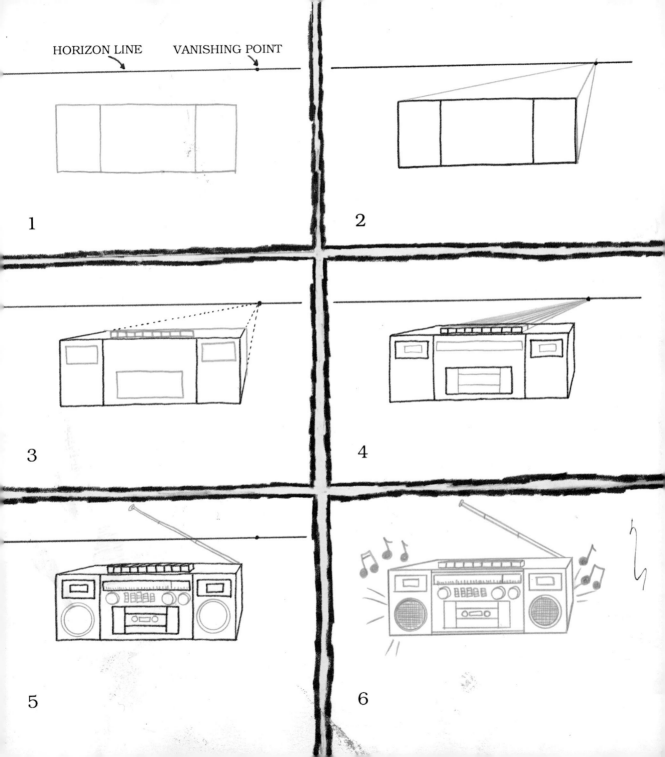

HORIZON LINE   VANISHING POINT

1

2

3

4

5

6

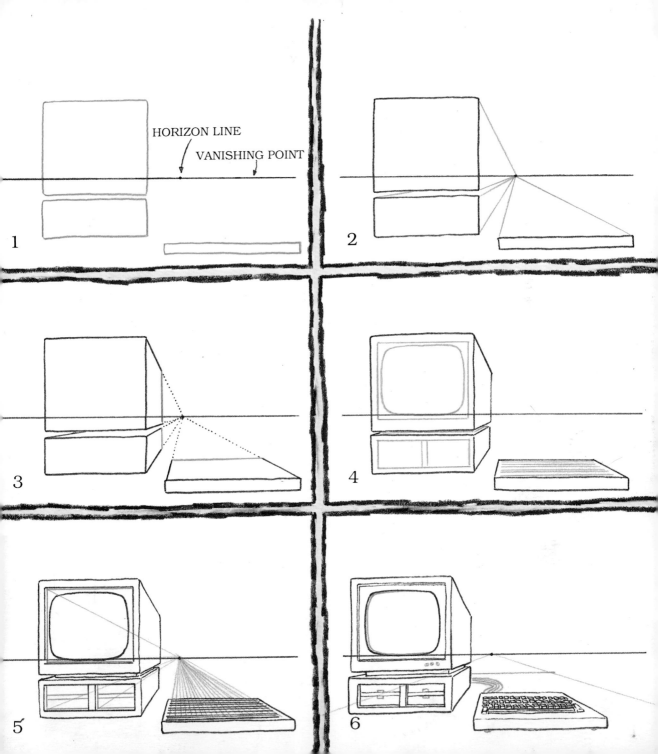

HORIZON LINE

VANISHING POINT

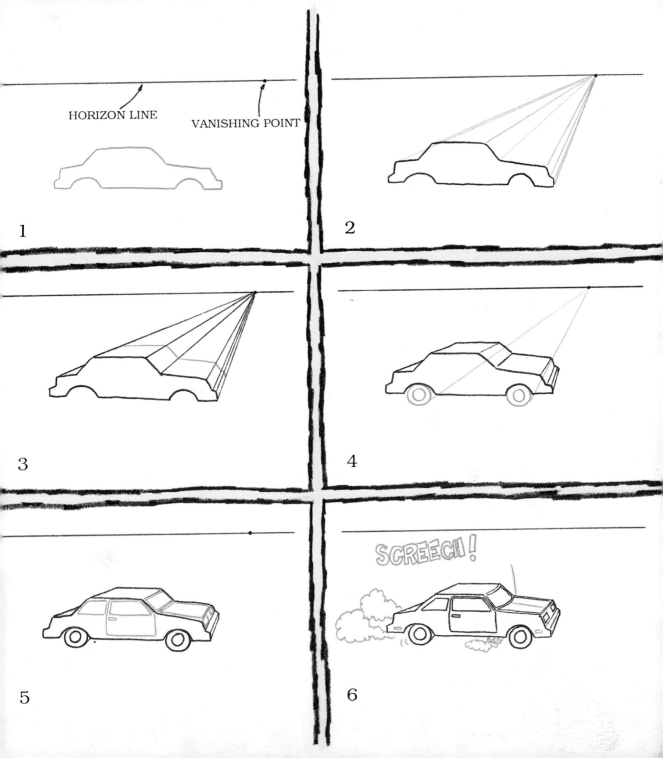

HORIZON LINE

VANISHING POINT

1

2

3

4

5

6

SCREECH!

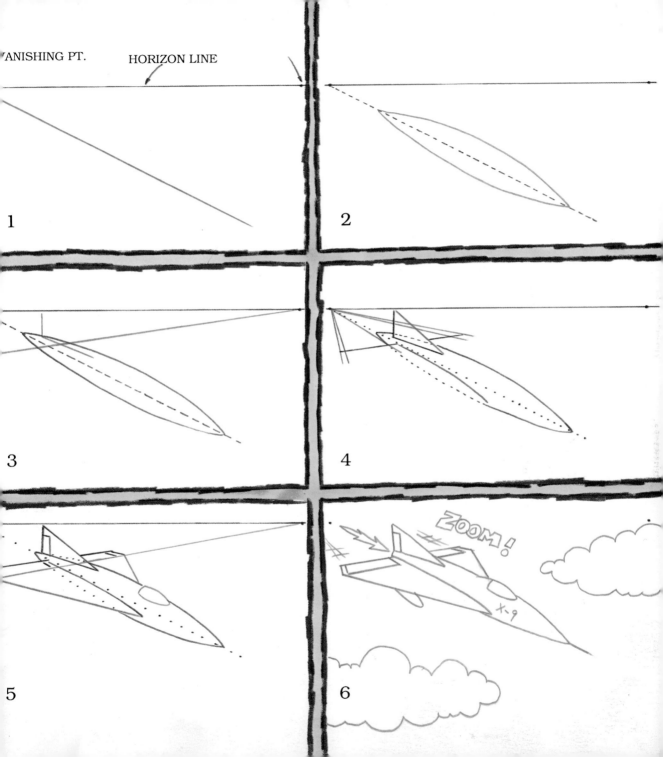

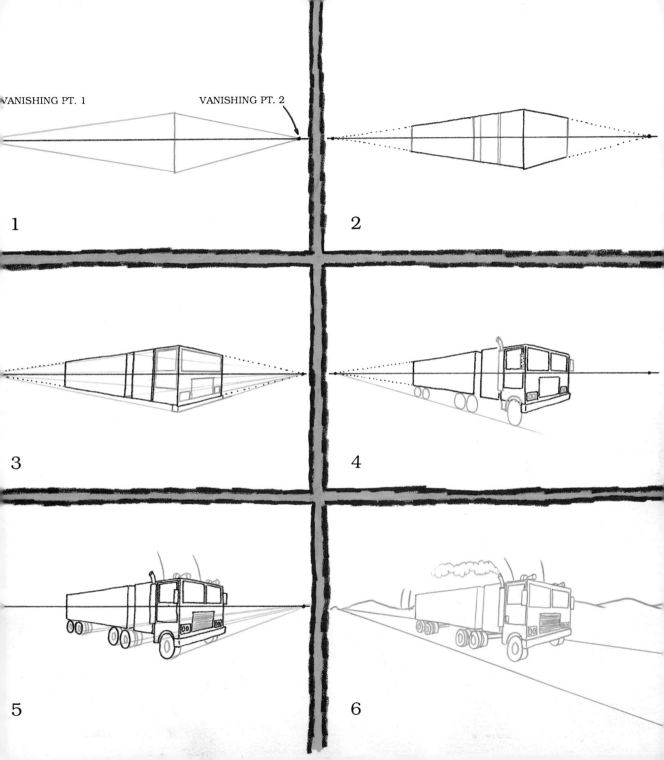

VANISHING PT. 1

VANISHING PT. 2

1

2

3

4

5

6